MW01226996

# Quick Start to using Essential Oils
## Foundational Concepts for Aromatherapy

1st Edition
2018
Deanna Russell, Clinical Aromatherapist, EOT®

Lone Flower Press

**Quick Start to using Essential Oils**
Foundational Concepts for Aromatherapy
Deanna Russell

This edition first published 2018

Font used: Lora

Cover photograph by Annie Spratt on Unsplash
Cover design by Deanna Russell
Illustrations are from Pixabay and public domain

Search key words: aromatherapy, essential oils, natural wellness

# Disclaimer Notice to Readers

The information contained in this book is not intended as a substitute for medical care and/or any medication prescribed to you by your health care provider. It is not meant to diagnose or replace treatment(s) by your health care provider. This book is for informational purposes only, and is sold with the understanding that neither the publisher nor the author shall be held liable or responsible for any loss, injury, or harm allegedly as a result from any information in this book.

Nature Notes nor Deanna Russell are responsible for any adverse effects or consequences resulting directly or indirectly from the use or misuse of essential oils, or any of the methods, recipes or suggestions outlined in this book.

This book is brand neutral.

The Food and Drug Administration (FDA) has not evaluated the statements contained in this book.

# About the author

Deanna Russell is a clinical aromatherapist, registered aromatherapist, and essential oil therapist (EOT®) located in Calgary, Alberta, Canada. She is an instructor passionate about educating people who want to use essential oils.
She is the owner and founder of Nature Notes Aromatherapy, and has a private consulting practice in Calgary, Canada.

Deanna is a professional member of BCAOA (British Columbia Alliance Of Aromatherapy) in Canada in good standing.

Deanna loves photography, design, gardening, tea blending, and typography. She has been experimenting and creating since early childhood, with plans to continue into very old age.

For information on and registration for aromatherapy on-line courses instructed by Deanna Russell, go to her website:
https://www.naturenote.ca

***Quick Start to Using Essential Oils*** is perfect for the person who is excited about using essential oils, especially the beginner. This handy reference book contains the information that you should have at the start of your essential oil journey. With all the practical tips included, you will refer to it often, even as you gain experience.

This book covers the foundational concepts you need to **get started quickly** using essential oils safely and effectively.
It is also the textbook for the Aromatherapy Foundational Concepts course taught by Deanna Russell.

# Contents

# Aromatherapy Terms

# What is aromatherapy, anyway?

**Quick Start:**
To get started, here are two excellent definitions of aromatherapy:

*Aromatherapy is the practice of using the natural oils extracted from flowers, bark, stems, leaves, roots or other parts of a plant to enhance psychological and physical well-being.*
www.aromatherapy.com

*"Aromatherapy is... the skilled and controlled use of essential oils for physical and emotional health and well being.*
Valerie Cooksley

Please pay special attention to the words "skilled" and "controlled use". It is important that you use essential oils respectfully.

Aromatherapy carries a much broader definition as well. This word has been tossed around to include other applications too.

**Beauty and perfume industries** use aromatherapy for marketing their scented products. You've seen this with dish soap, shampoos, body wash, shaving cream etc.
In commercially prepared products, the aromatherapy part is mostly synthetically recreated.

**Food industry** uses include aromatic tea blends. For example, bergamot is used in Earl Grey tea. Syrups are also now available using essential oils. Spearmint gum uses spearmint essential oil.

**Cosmetic specialists** use it in spa treatments. If you've been lucky enough to have an aromatherapy facial, or an aromatherapy massage, you know what I mean. Adding aromatherapy to your spa services is usually a luxury add-on component.

# What is aromatherapy, anyway?

**Self care products** use essential oils to enhance emotional wellbeing which in turn promotes improved immune responses. Essential oil blends are useful, and can be custom made.
This includes items such as diffuser blends, room sprays, lotions and creams, etc.

**Clinical Aromatherapy** is carried out by a trained professional with levels of certification.
This book does not cover these levels of instruction. It takes years to complete the requirements for this. The levels of certification can vary from country to country.

To locate a qualified aromatherapist in your area, check listings made available by professional associations in your country.
Several of these are listed for you in the resources section
(pages 106, 107).

This book will help you lay the foundation for using essential oils for yourself, family and friends.

**Quick Tip:**
When the food industry uses essential oils, they are using an oil that has been made safe for food consumption.
Words you might come across include "rectified" or "re-distilled oils".

**Quick Start:**
We cover ingestion of essential oils in the safety chapter.
"To eat, or not to eat..."
This is the question I am asked the most!

# What are essential oils?

## Quick Start: Definition of essential oils

I think the following defines essential oils quite nicely:

*"Pure essential oils are a product of distillation or expression (or other methods of extraction) of the aromatic substances, or essences, found in plants. The oils are volatile, which means they evaporate on exposure to air, and have a powerful aroma."*
Nerys Purchon & Lora Cantele

## Quick Tip:

Keep your essential oil bottles tightly closed to avoid evaporation!

Let's just talk about essential oils for a moment here.
They are volatile- which means that they will evaporate.

In real life this means that if you forget to cap your essential oil bottle, over time you will find some of it has gone missing- into thin air. This would be a most unpleasant surprise!
Your room might smell quite nice, but your oils will evaporate from the bottle if it has not been capped *tightly*.

I also want to mention that essential oils are oils, and they are **not** soluble in water.
Essential oils and water do not mix unless you add an emulsifier.

Most essential oils have some kind of an aroma, especially since they are the essence of the plant they represent. When we come to the blending chapter, you will see how plants are categorized to make pleasing aromatherapy blends using essential oils.

# What are essential oils?

**The main differences between essential oils and carrier oils**

*Essential oils:*
- are not water soluble
- evaporate when exposed to air
- are flammable
- highly aromatic
- very potent concentration of plant material
- direct topical application (neat) is not recommended for most
- are perfect for diffuser use

*Carrier oils:*
- have little or no aroma
- have a slow evaporation rate
- are used to dilute essential oils in order to apply topically safely
- are extracted from nuts, seeds of plants
- go rancid over time
- not water soluble
- contain nutrients and healing capabilities
- do not belong in a diffuser

Essential oils diluted in a carrier oil are the perfect way to extend the life of your precious investment for use as a massage or body oil.

**Quick Tip:**
Do you have an essential oil that is past its prime?

You can use it in a room spray or add some drops into your vacuum bag to freshen up your space.

**Examples of common carrier oils include:**
- sweet almond oil
- grapeseed oil
- avocado oil
- apricot kernel oil
- jojoba (liquid wax)
- rice bran oil
- more on pages 85-89

# Sensitization- what is it and why should I care?

## Quick Start Definition:

Sensitization is the gradual process of an allergy build up from overuse of a particular oil. Some essential oils are notorious sensitizers- such as clove, cinnamon, black pepper, lemon and sometimes trees like pine and cedarwood.

Next we're going to talk about sensitization. It's kind of a big word, but you do need to know what it is, and why it's necessary to be aware of what this problem can mean for you.

Some oils are known to cause rapid sensitization, such as clove. You can reduce your risk of sensitization by using oils diluted, and in appropriate amounts with appropriate dilution rates.

So- how does this apply to me and why should I care?

If you use an oil extensively (even over a shorter time), one day you may find that using that oil gives you a rash, or some other kind of problem. If you develop an allergy to an essential oil, you must stop using it. Even lavender can cause sensitization if you overuse it.

Sensitization can be indicated by a rash or other skin problem, such as skin falling off.

For your safety, dilution of essential oils is highly recommended.

# Sensitization- what is it and why should I care?

We will cover dilution in more detail in the safety chapter. For now, understand that diluted means putting your essential oil into a carrier oil before applying it onto your body.

Using oils in appropriate amounts is a good preventative measure against both sensitization and overdose. You don't want liberally pour oils onto your skin, as you might get too much on yourself, which can result in an overdose.

### Reduce your risk of an essential oil overdose:
Taking breaks from using essential oils for a period of time helps reduce your risk of sensitization.

Rotating the oils you use also helps (using different ones, not the same one all the time) minimize your risk.

Start with lower amounts of essential oil in your carrier oil, especially if you have:

• sensitive skin
• damaged skin
• a compromised immune system

### Quick Tip:
Diluting essential oils helps reduce the risk of an overdose.

### Quick Tip:
Locate dilution rate chart info in the safety section on page 40.

# Cost of essential oils: Influencing factors

**Quick Fact:**
Some of the most expensive essential oils include rose otto, rose absolute, sandalwood, jasmine, melissa (lemon balm), champaca, neroli, helichrysum (immortelle), tuberose-even cannabis!

Chamomile used to be an affordable oil, however, due to it's surging popularity, global supply and demand has driven the cost of this oil up dramatically.

**Buyer beware:**
If you see rose, sandalwood, jasmine or melissa for a "really good deal", it may be diluted, synthetically enhanced, or a fragrance oil.

Read the label carefully. Always purchase from a reliable supplier.

Many times I have had clients who want to custom order an essential oil. Most of the time the oils requested happen to be rare, exotic, and expensive. Most people are very surprised at how much some of these oils cost. Here is the lowdown on some of the factors which influence the cost of your oils:

**High yield vs low yield of the plant**
Some plants have a lot of oil to give up, like an orange.
The orange peel gives us a lot of oil. The cost of sweet orange is much less than a plant oil that has very little oil to give up. Melissa has very little yield, so you will pay a lot more money for melissa than you would for an orange oil.

**Crop failure**
If there's been flooding or drought in an area, these things affect the global availability and subsequently drives prices up.

**Political unrest**
Sometimes political climate can

# Cost of essential oils: Influencing factors

be a factor, particularly with oils like sandalwood and helichrysum. War torn countries may have less than ideal soil conditions as well.

## Global supply and demand

Chamomile used to be reasonably affordable. All of a sudden it became very popular, and as more and more people purchased it, less became available, which drove the price up. Chamomile is at least triple the price now than it was five to six years ago.

## Extraction method

This also will impact your cost. If you have a $CO_2$ extracted oil, you likely paid more for it. $CO_2$ distillation machines are not yet widely available, which means limited distillation batches. The cost of $CO_2$ extracted oils should start to come down as more of these machines become available for use.

## Boutique vs. mass produced

A family owned and operated farm may have higher overhead than a large operation with more operating capital. You will pay more for boutique oils.

## Status of your oil

Whether the oil was conventionally produced, wild crafted, or organically produced will affect your cost. Conventionally produced oils generally cost less.

It costs more money to produce an organic oil because of all the certification costs that go into the land and preparing the land as well. Organic pest control is also more labor intensive.

On average, you can expect to pay 20% more for organic essential oils.

# How we get essential oils

**Quick Start definition:**
Hydrosols are a byproduct of the distillation process and can be very useful on their own.
To be true, hydrosols must come right from the distillation of the plant material.

When you distill plants, two things that result are:
• the essential oil
• hydrosols

When you purchase a hydrosol with essential oils added back into it, they are called essential waters. They are more potent than the hydrosol, but less potent than the essential oil.

There are 5 main ways of extracting essential oils from plants. Here's the lowdown:

**Steam distillation method**
This method is the most common method of extraction of plants. The distillation method may include a water distillation or a steam distillation, or a combination of these methods.

The essential oil is the most powerful and aromatic part (essence) of the plant.
This is what you are getting when you purchase your small bottle of essential oils.

**Cold pressed method**
This is also known as the expressed oil method, which is the usual method used for extracting citrus from the peel. However, citrus oils can also be extracted using steam distillation.
If citrus oils are extracted using steam distillation, they are generally not photosensitive.
Details on phototoxic oils may be found on page 27.

# How we get essential oils

## Solvent extraction

When the solvent extraction method is used, absolutes are the final product. These methods are reserved for delicate flowers such as jasmine, neroli and rose. Absolutes are very potent and are usually reserved for perfume making.

## Enfleurage

This is the oldest method of extraction, and not really used today except in France. Very large amounts of plant matter are needed, as well as a lot of fat.

This, along with the time it takes to complete this type of extraction, makes it a largely unused method.

## CO2 extraction method

This newer technology allows for extraction at a much lower temperature. This increases the yield and quality of the essential oil being extracted. It increases the potency of the oil, and allows for quicker distillation times.

It is still an expensive method, but the price should come down as machines become more available.

## Super cool:

Watch a video on cold pressed extraction on a commercial level https://www.youtube.com/watch?v=ob5Vo2e4yP8

Pictured below: collection of essential oils from my steam distillation unit

Photo credit: Deanna Russell

# How to choose your essential oils

## Insider tip:
Since essential oils are not yet strictly regulated, "Therapeutic Grade" essential oil is a term that companies use to convey quality, and to set themselves apart from other oil companies.

If you are looking at an essential oil, and that essential oil was extracted properly from quality plant matter- it *is* of therapeutic grade.

This marketing phrase doesn't *automatically* denote authoritative, exclusive quality.

Please do not get hung up on whether or not the label says therapeutic grade essential oil.

## Quick Tip:
ALWAYS READ THE LABEL CAREFULLY!

What do I look for when I choose my own essential oils? Here's my checklist:

• The bottle should be a dark glass color to protect it from damaging light. Be wary if the bottle is clear glass, or plastic.
• It should have drip cap so that you can measure out drops individually.
• The label should have the name of the essential oil on it.
• It should also have the botanical name, or Latin name.
• It should actually say *essential oil* on the label.
• It should indicate the country of origin. It matters to me where the oil comes from. I also like to know how the oil was extracted- if it was steam distilled or cold expressed etc. If your oil is organic or wildcrafted (harvested from the wild) it will probably say so on the label. You can expect to pay more for organic oils.
• The name of the company selling the essential oil should be on the label. In Canada this is mandatory.
• It should also have the company address or phone number.

# How to choose your essential oils

• The volume of essential oil should be on the label. In Canada it will be a metric value, for example, 5ml, or 15ml, etc.

• It should say "not for ingestion" on the label. It may also have other appropriate cautions or warnings listed on the label.

## Insider tips:

First of all, pure and natural essential oils are NOT fragrance oils or perfume oils. If the label says either of these, or if the label doesn't specify that it is an essential oil, it is more than likely:

• **Synthetically enhanced**, or called "nature identical"

• **Diluted** with other oils of similar organic chemistry, but less expensive to produce.

• Your bottle may **contain some essential oil**, but there will be other things added to it. If you are simply looking for fragrance, this would definitely be an inexpensive option.

• **A blend of essential oils**, for example: lavandin which is actually a hybrid oil.

• **Soap grade** essential oils have little therapeutic value and should cost less than other oils. They are often indicated as such.

**Quick Tip:**
Infused herbal oils are different from essential oils - They are a macerated oil and should be labeled appropriately.

**Quick Tip:**
Essential oils eat away plastic, some faster than others.
Tea tree and marjoram are famous plastic eaters.
This is why you should never store essential oils in a plastic bottle.

# Routes of Application

## Quick Start
### Note on diffusers
If you live in a climate which is normally dry, you should not experience problems with your machine causing mold problems. However-
if you live in a humid climate, you may want to rethink your diffuser option. There have been some concerns concerning mold growth problems due to regular diffuser use.

## Quick Tip
### Choosing a diffuser
Look for a machine that will best meet your requirements. There are many kinds of diffusers available now. Consider features like auto shut off, timed cycles, intermittent use and square footage coverage. My personal favorite kinds are the ultrasonic nebulizing machines.

You've successfully purchased your quality essential oils. Now what? There are three main ways to use essential oils.
The first one is **topical application.**

This is a really nice way to use your oils. Some examples of topical application include use as a **body oil, bath oil** or **massage oil.**
You can also make your own signature **perfume.**
You can make your own **body spray** or a **body lotion.**
Items for **facial care** include cleansers, toners, moisturizers and scrubs.

The second route of application is **inhalation.**

The most common inhalation method is probably the **diffuser.** Many of you may have a diffuser already, and if you don't have one and wish to purchase one you now have many excellent options to choose from.

The **facial steam** is another lovely inhalation route.
I really like this idea if I'm coming

# Routes of Application

down with a cold or if I have some kind of a sinus problem. If you are unfamiliar with what a facial steam is or how to do one, you can watch my YouTube video. Depending what you put in your facial steam, you can also treat acne problems, and use it as a stress reliever at the same time.

**Steam shower application**
Some showers have a little tray where you can add your oil. I don't have that in my shower, but I wish that I did. Instead, I just add a couple of drops in the corner where the water doesn't go, and voilà-instant aromatherapy steam shower.
If I have a headache, or if I want to just wake up a little bit and have a fresh start to my day, then I use this simple application.

**Dry inhalation**
This means that you smell the aroma directly from the bottle.
You could also add a couple of drops onto a tissue and smell it from there.

A **room spray** is another inhalation method. It's fun way to use your oil in the room just to freshen it up, or to create a specific aromatic space.

The third route of application is the **internal route.**

We will not cover this route of application in this book.
For safety reasons, do not ingest your essential oils.

What do I mean by ingest them? This means don't eat them, and don't drink them. I realize this is a highly, highly controversial topic, and that's why we're going to cover it in more detail later in the safety chapter.

**Quick How To**
**Face Steam Video**
https://www.YouTube.com/watch?v=iK_jF8FpLE0&t=1s

# Storage and Shelf Life of essential oils

**Quick Tip: safety**
*Always* store your essential oils away from the reach of children.

Some oils are definitely not safe to ingest. Eucalyptus is a good example of this.
It only takes a small amount to make someone very unwell– or even more tragically, result in a death.

Symptoms of eucalyptus poisoning include:
• labored breathing
• vomiting
• rash
• nausea

It's a good idea to keep the phone number for your local poison control nearby.

Proper storage of your essential oils is necessary to ensure that they stay their best for as long as possible. Essential oils should be stored:
• in a cool and dark place
• in dark glass bottles with an appropriate cap, usually drip cap
• your own blends should be labeled with all the ingredients and date you prepared it
• always, always keep your essential oils safely out of the reach of children
• store away from heat sources as essential oils are flammable
• store away from homeopathic remedies

How long you can expect your essential oils to last:

**Citrus:**
9-12 months. If stored in cool temperatures you might squeeze out a few additional months.

**Steam Distilled Oils:**
2-3 years on average with some exceptions.
Exceptions include tea tree, pine, and cypress. Expect these to last anywhere from 1- 16 months.

# Storage and Shelf Life of essential oils

Some steam distilled oils will age very gracefully such as patchouli and sandalwood.

**Co2 Extracted Oils:**
This method produces an oil which can last 5 years or longer.

**Absolutes:**
Absolutes generally last between 3-5 years.

**Extracts:**
These oils are used for aromatic cooking. It's harder to find them, but they do exist. They will be labeled accordingly. Don't use extracts in your diffuser, or to make blends. They are formulated for taste, not therapeutic value. They will have quite a long shelf life.

If you think your essential oil is past its prime, do not apply it to your skin. Use it as a room freshener or part of your cleaning solution instead.

**Quick Tip:**
The beauty of CO2 extracted oils is that you can get some really interesting ones.
For example:

• Rosehip seed extract
• Arnica flower extract
• Chia seed extract
• Lilac extract
• Turmeric extract
• Seabuckthorn extract

# Aromatherapy
# Safety

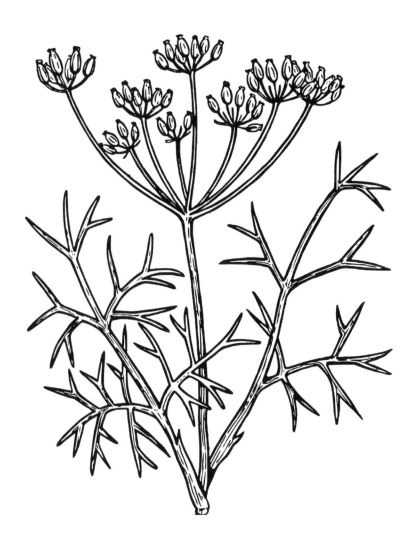

# Essential Oils General Safety Guidelines

Although essential oils are very powerful and useful, you should not depend upon them as your primary treatment for a serious condition. Essential oils should be regarded as a supplementary treatment, *not* as a replacement treatment.

Having said that- essential oils can be a very useful addition to your supplemental therapy and care, and you should feel free to choose a clinical aromatherapist as part of your team of care providers. An aromatherapy practitioner who is knowledgeable in their field can be of real benefit to you when dealing with psychological or physical health issues.
Holistic physicians can guide you through your treatment program. In fact, many allopathic (that is, conventional) doctors are open to supplemental therapy such as aromatherapy. You have nothing to lose by asking! In any event, always inform your doctor of your choices. They need to know.

Even though essential oils come from nature, it's still *possible to have an allergy* to them. It's important to be aware of this.
Also, *results and benefits from using essential oils can vary from person to person and are not guaranteed.*
This means that it could take you a few different attempts of custom blending to find something that's going to work for you based on your current needs and situation.

In general, **don't apply essential oils undiluted to your skin.**
Dilute them into a carrier oil before you applying essential oils topically. This will reduce your chances of sensitization and skin irritation. Also, by diluting essential oils, your investment will last longer. Exceptions to this would be would be in a first aid situation. Lavender and tea tree are the two generally accepted oils that you can apply neat -that is undiluted- to the skin.

# Essential Oils General Safety Guidelines

However, I recommend diluting even these oils, especially if you have sensitive skin.

**Rotate the oils that you use.**
You don't want to use the same oils over and over again. If you do that, the essential oil can lose its effectiveness for you, or, you may develop a sensitization to it. Lavender is an excellent example of this.
A lot of people use lavender for insomnia. It generally works very well as a sleep aid, so people continue using it. Then all of a sudden one night they discover that it is not working anymore. My suggestion- stop using it for a couple of weeks and then try using it again.

If you've developed a *sensitization* to lavender however, then you won't be able to use it anymore. So do your due diligence and reduce your risk of sensitization by rotating your oils -and besides, variety is the spice of life.

**Quick Start: How To**
Do a patch test

To check if you have a sensitivity to an essential oil, mix a couple of drops of the oil into a carrier oil and apply it to the inside of your elbow. Leave it for a day or so, and then check to see if you have any irritation.

If you discover that oil to be unfriendly to your skin, apply more carrier oil ONLY to the affected area to help dissipate it, and then wash carefully using soap and warm water.

# Essential Oils General Safety Guidelines

**Be aware of oils that are phototoxic or possibly phototoxic**
The word phototoxic describes what happens to you when you use an oil and then go out in the sunshine, and as a result, get a severe sunburn. In short, it increases your sensitivity to the sun, but it can also increase your risk of skin cancer.

**Be aware of known skin irritants**
A big one here is clove. Another oil that's known to be an irritant is cinnamon. It could be anything for you. So, if you notice that you have a problem with an oil, make note of it. Geranium is generally non irritating, but I know someone who has a problem using it, even one drop.

Here's the big issue that you've all been wondering about.

**Don't ingest essential oils**
Certain essential oils are toxic and can cause bodily harm if taken internally. A good example of this is eucalyptus.
I referred to this earlier. There have been recorded fatalities involving ingesting eucalyptus oil and sometimes it doesn't take a lot to make you very, very sick. So please don't ingest oils, especially eucalyptus. *Keep oils out of the reach of children.*

Essential oils are potent and some may burn or irritate your digestive tract on the way down. Oregano is a good example of this. Some who have tried ingesting oregano have already found this out for themselves. Remember, essential oils and water don't mix. If you add a drop of oregano to a glass of water, you are still going to get that burning feeling all the way down. The food industry uses essential oils, but they have certain elements extracted to make them safe for for public consumption. Peppermint and spearmint are examples of this.

# Essential Oils General Safety Guidelines

Please understand that I am not against ingesting essential oils per se- but it must be done under the supervision of an experienced professional who is specifically trained and qualified in this area.

**Ventilated environment**
Be careful not to overexpose yourself to essential oils when you are working with them.
Work in a well-ventilated area and take fresh air breaks often.
Some essential oils might induce a headache. For me, this includes jasmine. I am able to work with jasmine for a short while, and then I have to take some fresh air.

You might experience a type of toxic buildup if you over expose yourself to essential oils. Some signs that indicate you need to rest from using essential oils include:
• headache
• nausea
• skin irritation
• the feeling that it's been "too much for you".

**Quick insight:**
Recently I was speaking with a traveler from Europe about essential oils. He was very excited to let me know how he was eating them using sugar as a carrier. The problem was, he had been eating eucalyptus (among others).

He looked a little frightened when I explained the danger of doing this.
He hadn't known that eucalyptus is toxic when ingested. *The biggest problem I see is that people are eating oils without knowing about their safety.*

I suggested he use it (eucalyptus) in the shower instead, solving his sinus problem in a safer, yet effective way.

# Using Essential Oils
## during pregnancy and postpartum

There are some special things that you need to know when using essential oils during pregnancy and postpartum. The first thing that I'd like to recommend is to stay away from using any essential oils at all during the first trimester, especially if you have a history of miscarriage, or if this is your first pregnancy and you do not know how your body will respond to essential oils. (Using a little ginger in a diffuser is okay.)
After the first trimester is safely passed, you can start experimenting with certain essential oils using them highly diluted. Citrus essential oils are among the safest ones, along with lavender and Roman chamomile.

There is quite a lot of controversy surrounding safety of essential oils during pregnancy. You'll notice that even different books will disagree about which oils are safe or not safe. If you are uncertain about using an essential oil, or if you have *any* concerns about it- simply don't use it. You can wait until after the birth. There will be plenty of time after your baby is born to enjoy these oils again.

Peppermint and sage are two essential oils that you should not use if you are breastfeeding, as they have been known to dry up milk supply.
However, if your goal is to dry up your milk supply, by all means go ahead and use these.
When you are ready to use essential oils on your little one, I would suggest waiting for at least a couple of weeks to a month, or even six weeks after they are born.
You want to form an attachment with your baby, and the best way that you can do that is to have your own smell. If you always smell like an essential oil, your baby won't get to know *your unique smell.* A baby's sense of smell is much more delicate than your own as well, another thing to keep in mind.

# Using Essential Oils
## during pregnancy and postpartum

**Safest oils to use after the first trimester has passed (Uncomplicated pregnancy)**

- Petitgrain
- Geranium
- Lavender-after 6 months
- Neroli (after 6 months)
- Sandalwood
- Rose (after 6 months)
- Ylang ylang
- Citrus oils

Using essential oils after a vaginal birth provides multiple benefits. They may be added to Epsom salts and dissolved into warm bath water to **ease pain** and help **prevent infection**. Perhaps even more importantly, the oils are also **relaxing** and **stress reducing**.

Try lavender and tea tree for infection prevention.
If you have rose, now is the time to use a drop or two. I'd use it with frankincense, or any of the oils listed above.

**Quick Tip: labor**
Certain essential oils are very useful during labor, for example, jasmine or clary sage. These oils can induce uterine contractions, and make them more effective, possibly resulting in shorter and more efficient labor.

Clary sage and jasmine are also helpful for postpartum recovery. These oils are particularly helpful in dealing with pain, or any kind of emotional trauma that you may have had during the birth, as well as helping deal with postpartum depression.

# Avoid these: toxic essential oils

Avoiding these toxic oils shouldn't be too difficult- most of them are not readily available.

Ajowan
Bitter almond
Arnica
Basil, exotic
Boldo Leaf
Buchu
Calamus
Camphor, yellow
Cassia
Chervil
Deertongue
Elecampane
Horseradish
Jaborandi
Melilotus
Mugwort
Mustard
Nutmeg
Pennyroyal
Parsley
Pine, dwarf
Rue
Sage, common
Santolina
Saffras Savin/Savine Savoury
Narcissus
Spanish broom
Snakeroot
Tansy
Thuja
Tonka
Wintergreen
Wormseed
Wormwood

# Avoid these: irritant and phototoxic oils

## Avoid possible skin irritants:

Angelica
Aniseed
Basil
Benzoin
Birch
Black pepper
Cassia
Cedarwood
Cinnamon bark
Citronella
Clove
Coriander
Elemi
Fennel
Fir needle
Ginger
Hyssop
Lemon
Lemongrass
Lime
Manuka
Melissa
Myrtle
Nutmeg
Oregano
Peppermint, Spearmint
Thyme

Be sure to highly dilute these oils if you want to apply them topically.

## Phototoxic Essential Oils

Angelica root
Bergamot
Celery
Cumin
Ginger
Grapefruit, white
Lemon
Lemon eucalyptus
Lemon verbena
Lime
Mandarin
Melissa
Orange, bitter
Parsnip
Rue
Tangerine
Verbena

Application of one of these oils before sun exposure will increase your sensitivity to the sun and greatly increase your risk of sunburn.

Save these for use at night if you want to apply them, especially topically.

# Aromatherapy and Cancer Care

I wanted to include an expanded section on cancer care and aromatherapy. For those of you who have had your life changed in a heartbeat and in a way that you did not plan for, you might be feeling a lot of different things.

You might feel shocked- like this can't be happening to you, or be unable to focus on things. You might be worried about making future plans. You might be feeling angry and frustrated and helpless and terrified. You may be in pain, and you might feel very, very alone.

I'd like to cover a couple of different things you can do if you want to use essential oils during your treatments.

## Using a diffuser

Be sure to put less oil into your diffuser and only run it 10 minutes out of the hour. You don't need to run the machine at full steam. You might be sensitive to smell, especially during rounds of chemotherapy. Some people lose their sense of smell for awhile entirely for a period of time.

## Topical Application

If you plan to use essential oils topically, be sure use them highly diluted, especially if you have been doing radiation treatments and your skin has been burned. Make sure only organic essential oils, and organic carrier oils are used.

I highly recommend that if you want to do this that you work with a qualified aromatherapist. You should have someone specialized in this field to help you do it properly and to ensure the essential oils you are using are suitable to your individual needs.

## Talk to your doctor

I highly recommend having a discussion with your doctor about using essential oils during your treatment. Some essential oils

# Aromatherapy and Cancer Care

interact with medications, and chemotherapy drugs. While a lot of people want to take ginger for nausea, be sure to check with your doctor to make sure that it's not going to conflict with any other medications that you're currently taking. It is also recommended to stop using ginger two weeks before and after surgeries due to its blood thinning properties.

Additionally there are certain essential oils that you should not be using during this time.
If you have **any type of cancer** you should **not use**:

• Aniseed
• Basil
• Bay laurel
• Cinnamon
• Clove
• Fennel
• Ho leaf
• Nutmeg
• Star anise

These oils are known to have some hormone altering properties. You don't want that to be a cause for concern in your care at this time.

**Quick Tip**
Your sense of smell will likely be affected during chemotherapy treatments.

Don't eat your favorite foods or use your essential oils for a few days before and after chemotherapy treatments. Why? You don't want to create a negative association with using those things by the way they smell and the way that they make you feel.

Have an alternate plan for treatment days and save your favorite things for when you are feeling a little bit better.

# Cancers Affecting Men

Examples of this type of cancer include:

• Prostate
• Testicular
• Penile

If you have a male specific cancer, you should be avoiding all the previously mentioned oils in the general cancer section, plus the following:

• Angelica
• Basil
• Combova
• Hyssop
• Mastic
• Pine
• Rose geranium
• Wild thyme

# Estrogen Dependent Cancers

If you have a female specific cancer, you should be avoiding all the previously mentioned oils in the general cancer section, plus the following:

• Angelica
• Blue tansy
• Clary sage, all types of sage
• Cypress
• Coriander
• Cajeput
• Combova
• Cumin
• Hops
• Lemongrass
• Lovage
• Ravensara anisata
• Verbena

Examples of this type of cancer include:

• Uterine
• Breast
• Ovarian

# Practical Tips during cancer treatments

I want to point out here that aromatherapy can be an effective and important part of your care and recovery program. Studies have shown that aromatherapy can significantly impact the emotional well-being of a cancer patient. Here are some reasons why aromatherapy can be helpful:

• Aromatherapy helps people cope with insomnia, pain, and chemotherapy induced nausea.
• Aromatherapy can help you get your appetite back.
• Aromatherapy can help you relax, and more importantly, it may help you fight off feelings of depression.

All these benefits affect your immune system, which in turn affects your ability to recover.
Studies have shown that your mental state of mind is directly linked with your body's immune system.
You definitely want to promote all the possibilities of recovery. You want your body to have the best chance possible to fight this disease and win.

**Mood lifting** essential oils include:
Mandarin, lemon balm and orange.

Lemon balm is also known as melissa essential oil, and it is actually quite expensive. That may be a factor when you are creating an essential oil blend, but mandarin and orange make excellent substitutes and they are very accessible and much more affordable.

**Painkilling, Pain reducing** (analgesic) oils:
Chamomile, lavender, peppermint, rosewood.

# Practical Tips during cancer treatments

**Calming** essential oils include: Chamomile, lavender, patchouli, rosewood.

**Relaxing** essential oils include: Black spruce, cedarwood, fir and ylang ylang.

Note that pine is not included on this list. It is contraindicated for male specific cancers.

**Stimulating** essential oils:
Bergamot (also uplifting)
Jasmine (also relaxing)
Geranium
Cardamom
Orange (sweet)
Tea tree

Stimulating essential oils can be very useful when you feel like you need to get your appetite back. Remember, you do not want to stop eating. You need to have proper nutrition during this time. Even though you may not be eating much at all, your food choices matter a great deal more.

**Quick Tip:**
Lavender and chamomile go very nicely together. Try a ratio of 3:1.

3 drops lavender
1 drop chamomile

**Pro Tip:**
Bergamot is at the top of my list because it is also uplifting; a natural depression fighter.

# Other Medical Conditions

## Epilepsy & Seizures

If you have epilepsy or seizures avoid:

• Hyssop
• Rosemary
• Sage (all types)
• Sweet fennel

## Glaucoma

If you have glaucoma avoid:

• Cypress
• Hyssop
• Listea cubeba
  (May chang)
• Thyme

## High Blood Pressure

If you have high blood pressure, it's generally accepted in the aromatherapy community to avoid using:
• Pine
• Rosemary
• Sage (all types)
• Thyme
You may come across conflicting information when checking various lists.

## Low Blood Pressure

If you have low blood pressure avoid:

• Clary sage
• Lavender
• Lemon
• Sweet marjoram
• Yarrow
• Ylang ylang

## Tip:

You can use lavender and sweet marjoram to help bring your blood pressure down.

# Other Medical Conditions

**Impaired Kidney Function**
If you have kidney damage, or are missing a kidney, avoid:

• Anise
• Birch tar
• Juniper berry
• Wintergreen
*plus all toxic essential oils

Make sure that, when you are using essential oils in general, that you stay well hydrated to avoid further damaging your kidneys.

**Do not use with homeopathic remedies:**

• Black pepper
• Eucalyptus
• Peppermint

**Quick Tip**
When storing your homeopathic remedies and flower essences, be sure to keep them well separated from any powerful aromatics, including coffee.

# Dilution Rates & Contraindications

# Contraindications Chart

In this section we're going to look at contraindication and calculation and dilution rate charts. What these charts allow you to do is determine beforehand what essential oils you should not be using and the reason(s) why.

Things that you want to include on your contraindication chart:
- pregnancy
- high or low blood pressure, etc.

Make a note of *all* essential oils that are contraindicated for you and for each person that you will be blending for. It's best to have a chart for each member of the family so that you can keep everyone organized.

The next thing that you should know is that the dilution rate is standard at 2 percent to 3 percent. You can go as high as 4 percent for a total body massage oil.

Refer to the calculation chart for easy calculation of dilution rates so that you can know how many drops per mil or teaspoon or ounce that you want to use.

Your carrier oil can be your choice between grapeseed oil or apricot kernel or sweet almond oil or even coconut oil, if that's what you prefer. You just need to have an oil to carry your essential oils before you put it onto your skin.

For additional information on carrier oils, go to page 85.

You should also make a note of the health of your skin. If your skin has eczema or psoriasis, or if it is damaged in some way, you will want to use less essential oils due to the compromised condition of your skin.

# Contraindications Chart

The other thing that you should do now is to keep track of your blending formulas. There is nothing more frustrating than experimenting with essential oils and formulating the perfect solution for you- only to forget how you did it when you go to remake it later.

I confess this has happened to me, and more than once! Make sure that you write down the botanical name of the essential oils that you use, and how many drops of each.

It's also helpful to make notes on how helpful it is to you-or not. If it works for you, you can easily recreate your project, and if it does not work for you, then you would know to not make it again. I also keep track of any reactions such as skin irritation etc.

You could also record the emotional outcome here as well.

**Quick Tip:**
Contraindication refers to "something (such as a symptom or condition) that makes a particular treatment or procedure inadvisable" Merriam Webster dictionary

**Quick Start:**
A standard dilution rate is 10 drops of essential oils total in four teaspoons or 20 mils of your carrier oil. So -you will select a total of 10 essential oil drops. It can be a combination of whatever drops that you want but *do not* exceed the 10 drops.

**Example:**

4 tsp sunflower oil
3 drops lavender
2 drops eucalyptus
3 drops rosemary
2 drops peppermint

# Contraindications Chart Example

Date: _____
List of contraindications essential oils for: _____

Name of oil: _____ Reason: _____
Name of oil: _____ Reason: _____
Name of oil: _____ Reason: _____
Name of oil: _____ Reason: _____
Name of oil: _____ Reason: _____
Name of oil: _____ Reason: _____
Name of oil: _____ Reason: _____
Name of oil: _____ Reason: _____
Name of oil: _____ Reason: _____
Name of oil: _____ Reason: _____
Name of oil: _____ Reason: _____
Name of oil: _____ Reason: _____
Name of oil: _____ Reason: _____
Name of oil: _____ Reason: _____

## Dilution Chart

| Dilution Rate | # of drops | Per oz/ml carrier |
| --- | --- | --- |
| 1% | 5-6 | 1 oz/30ml |
| 2% | 10-12 | 1 oz/30ml |
| 3% | 15-18 | 1 oz/30ml |

# Quick References

On average, there are about 20 drops of essential oil in a mil. This is based on a standard drip size in North America. Other countries may use a smaller drip size, in which case the average would be more like 24-25 drops per mil. For the purposes of this book, we are working with the 20 drops per mil average.

## General Usage Guidelines

Babies: use 0.5%
Children: use 1-1.5%
Elderly and/or frail: use 1-1.5%
Pregnancy: use 1-2%
Standard: use 3%
Therapeutic targeted area: use 4-10%

Find more detailed information of the dilutions rates for babies and children in the recipes section, page 94.

## Dilution Chart

| Dilution Rate | # of drops | Per oz/ml carrier |
|---------------|------------|-------------------|
| 1% | 10-12 | 2 oz/60ml |
| 2% | 20-24 | 2 oz/60ml |
| 3% | 30-36 | 2 oz/60ml |

# Classification

# Classification of Essential Oils

| Trees, Woods & Shrubs | Grasses, Seeds & Roots |
|---|---|
| Bay laurel | Angelica root |
| Birch | Carrot seed |
| Cajeput | Citronella |
| Cedarwood | Ginger root |
| Cypress | Helichrysum |
| Eucalyptus | Lemongrass |
| Fir balsam | Palmarosa |
| Juniper berry | Vetiver |
| Listea cubeba | |
| Manuka | |
| Myrtle | |
| Niaouli | |
| Palo santo | |
| Patchouli | |
| Petitgrain | |
| Pine | |
| Ravensara | |
| Rosewood | |
| Sandalwood | |
| Spruce | |
| Tea tree | |

# Classification of Essential Oils

## Herbs

Basil
Clary sage
Fennel, sweet
Hyssop
Lemon verbena
Marjoram, sweet
Melissa (lemon balm)
Oregano
Peppermint
Rosemary
Sage
Spearmint
Thyme
Yarrow

## Quick Tip

Did you know?
The bitter orange tree
(Citrus aurantium)
produces three different
types of essential oils.

**Neroli** is produced from
the flowers of the tree. It
is one of the most
expensive oils available
due to the amount of
flowers required to
produce 1 pound of
essential oil (1,000 lbs+).

**Petitgrain** is produced
from the leaves and twigs.

**Orange** is produced from
the peel.

# Classification of Essential Oils

## Citrus

Bergamot
Grapefruit
Lemon
Lime
Mandarin
Sweet orange
Blood orange
Bitter orange
Tangerine
Yuzu

## Oleoresins

Benzoin
Capsicum
Cassia
Clove
Copiaba
Ginger root
Nutmeg
Vanilla

Dictionary Definition of
Oleoresins: "a natural plant
product containing chiefly
essential oil and resin."
They are mainly used in the
food and baking industries,
but are also used medicinally.

## Flowers & Exotics

Carnation absolute
Champaca
Chamomile German
Chamomile Roman
Geranium
Hyacinth absolute
Lavender
Linden Blossom
Lotus flower absolute
Marigold absolute
Narcissus absolute
Osmanthus
Rose geranium
Rose otto
Rose absolute
Neroli
Jasmine
Tuberose absolute
Violet leaf
Ylang ylang

# Classification of Essential Oils

## Gums & Resins

Benzoin
Frankincense
Galbanum
Myrrh

## Spices

Allspice
Black pepper
Cardamom
Caraway
Cinnamon bark, leaf
Clove bud
Coriander
Cumin
Nutmeg
Turmeric

# Most Common Botanical Family Groupings

## Labiatae

Basil
Clary sage
Hyssop
Lavender
Marjoram
Melissa
Oregano
Patchouli
Peppermint
Rosemary
Sage
Spearmint
Thyme

## Rutaceae

Bergamot
Buchu
Grapefruit
Lemon
Lime
Mandarin
Neroli
Orange
Petitgrain
Rue
Tangerine
Yuzu

## Zingiberaceae

Cardamom
Galangal
Ginger root
Saffron
Turmeric

## Gramineae/Poaceae

Citronella
Gingergrass
Lemongrass
Palmarosa
Vetiver

# Most Common Botanical Family Groupings

## Compositae/Asterceae

German chamomile
Roman chamomile
Helichrysum
Yarrow

## Myrtaceae

Cajeput
Clove bud
Eucalyptus
Manuka
Myrtle
Honey myrtle
Niaouli
Tea tree

## Umbelliferae

Angelica
Anise
Celery
Coriander
Cumin
Carrot seed
Dill
Fennel
Lovage

## Lauraceae

Bay laurel
Cinnamon
Listea cubeba
Ravensara
Rosewood

## Cupressaceae

Cypress
Juniper berry
Thuja

## Pinaceae

Cedarwood
Fir
Pine
Spruce

# Blending
# Essential Oils

# Blending Wheel

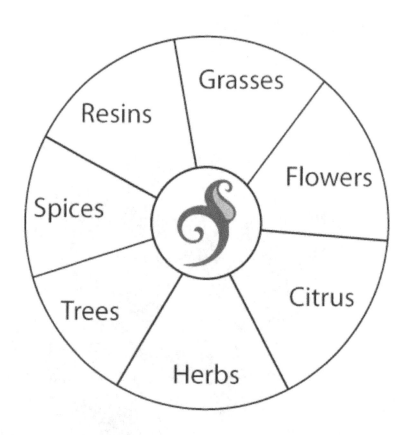

# Blending Essential Oils

## What you need to know about using a blending wheel

### #1 Blending Tip:
All of the oils in each category go with each other.
For example, all the trees go together. All the herbs- go together. All the citrus -you can blend together.

In **citrus** groupings:
You can mix up lemon with lime, no problem.

In **spice** groupings:
You can mix up clove with cinnamon, no problem.

In **floral** groupings:
You can mix geranium with lavender, no problem.

### #2 Blending Tip:
Here's the second thing that you should know about the blending wheel:
Each of the sections on the wheel go with the one next to it. This means that you can blend a flower with a grass, or a tree with a herb.

### Blending with adjacent groups
Lemon (citrus) + lavender (flower)

Lavender (flower) + spruce (tree)

Cinnamon leaf (spice) + frankincense (resin)

Ginger root (grasses and roots) + ylang ylang (flower)

# Making a Harmonious Blend

Essential oils have been categorized into notes, as in perfumery or music.

When oils are combined with balance in mind the results can be not only effective, but lovely, too.

## Pro Tip:
Jeanne Rose has an easy to remember blending tip:

5 drops base note
10 drops middle notes
20 drops top notes

## Quick Tip:
When inhaling aromas one after the next, the senses may become over-whelmed and smells may lose their definition.

Smelling some fresh coffee beans will act as a reset button for the nose. This is an effective (and pleasant) way to cleanse the nose palette.

Some people start at the top and add each note until they form a perfect chord, usually ending with a bass note.
Some people also start at the bottom (at the base) and build up their chord from there.

Either way is fine- It just depends on your personal preference.

## What is a top note?
A top note hits the nose first, but then the aroma is short lived. This is generally a bright, lively, or sharp aroma.

## Middle Note
Middle notes make up the bulk of your overall combination.
They add texture and interest to a blend. There is often more than one middle note in a blend.

**Bass notes** anchor the scent and have longer staying power.

Typically, there are more top notes in a blend than bass notes.

# Blending Notes

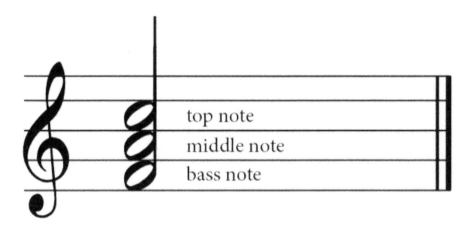

top note
middle note
bass note

## Quick Start Blending tips:

Try blending essential oils within the same group together. Or, try mixing oils with the neighboring list, as shown on the blending wheel.
To start, keep your plans simple, using two or three essential oils. When you get more experience, you can have three or four, or even five.

Please be aware of essential oil safety issues and plan accordingly. This is where your contraindication chart will come in handy.

Try balancing scents using a combination of top middle and bass notes. Some essential oils have a more powerful or delicate note and some linger more than others. This is where experimenting gets really fun.

For example, bergamot will hit your nose first, but then it will fade away sooner, whereas patchouli will linger for quite some time.

# Note Classification Categories

| Top Notes | Middle Notes | Base Notes |
|---|---|---|
| Basil | Angelica | Benzoin |
| Bergamot | Black pepper | Cedarwood |
| Cajeput | Carrot seed | Champaca |
| Cardamom | Chamomiles | Cinnamon leaf |
| Citronella | Coriander | Clove |
| Cumin | Cypress | Frankincense |
| Eucalyptus (all) | Fennel (sweet) | Helichrysum |
| Ginger | Fir | Jasmine |
| Grapefruit | Geranium | Myrrh |
| Lemon | Hyssop | Neroli |
| Lemongrass | Juniper berry | Patchouli |
| Lime | Lavender | Rose |
| Mandarin | Manuka | Sandalwood |
| Niaouli | Marjoram | Vanilla |
| Orange | Melissa | Ylang ylang |
| Palmarosa | Myrtle | |
| Petitgrain | Oregano | |
| Sage | Peppermint | |
| Tea tree | Pine | |
| Thyme | Ravensara | |
| Yarrow | Rosalina | |
| | Rosemary | |
| | Rosewood | |
| | Spearmint | |
| | Spruce | |

# Quick Start Blending Charts

Use the blending chart example below to help you organize your blending ideas. Refer to the following for examples of how this chart can be used.

## Blending Worksheet Chart

| Name of oil | Bass note | Middle note | Top note | Grouping |
|---|---|---|---|---|
|  |  |  |  |  |
|  |  |  |  |  |
|  |  |  |  |  |
| name of blend: |  |  |  |  |

## Blending with adjacent groups starting with top note

| Name of oil | Top note | Middle note | Bass note | Grouping |
|---|---|---|---|---|
| ginger | 2 drops |  |  | grasses/root |
| lavender |  | 2 drops |  | flower |
| vetiver |  |  | 1 drop | grass |
| name of blend: |  |  |  |  |

## Blending within the same grouping starting with bass note

| Name of oil | Bass note | Middle note | Top note | Grouping |
|---|---|---|---|---|
| patchouli | 1 drop |  |  | shrub/tree |
| cypress |  | 2 drops |  | shrub/tree |
| tea tree |  |  | 2 drops | shrub/tree |
| name of blend: |  |  |  |  |

# Essential Oil Profiles

# Bergamot
*Citrus bergemia*

## Quick Start
Top note
Family: Rutaceae
Extraction method: cold pressed
Country of origin: Italy
Price range: reasonably inexpensive
Safety notes:
Child friendly over age 6 and pregnancy friendly
Possible skin irritant- use diluted
Bergamot is also extremely phototoxic unless labeled as FCF, which means furocoumarin free. During processing, the furocoumarin is extracted from the oil, rendering it safer for exposure to the sun.
Since bergamot is more phototoxic than other citrus, waiting for 24-72 hours before sun exposure is advised.

## Practical Tips and uses for Bergamot
One of the reasons why I like bergamot is because it's a good disinfectant. It's **anti-bacterial**. You can use this oil if you want to make a cleaning product for your bathroom or kitchen. It smells wonderful, even all by itself.

Like most citrus, bergamot is a good **digestion aid**. It's an **expectorant**, an **antiviral** and it's **calming**.

Bergamot is widely used in **uplifting** aromatherapy formulas. In fact, it is used to treat mild and moderate depression, including seasonal affective disorder (SAD). If you are using bergamot to treat a depressed state, and it is not working for you, you should seek professional help. However, if you have a mild to moderate case, it can be really useful, and an appropriate place to start.

# Bergamot
*Citrus bergemia*

## Skin Care Uses

Because Bergamot is so anti-bacterial it is effective for skin problems like **acne.**
It is often used in face care products for **oily skin**.

One of the best ways you can use this is either in a facial steam for acne, or if you have the FCF version you can use it in a skin care preparation for use during the daytime. Otherwise keep it for use at night.

Try bergamot for skin conditions such as **psoriasis, eczema, itchy skin,** and **scabies**.

Bottom line- I definitely recommend having this oil. Bergamot is anti-viral, and very useful in banishing germs during the cold and flu season.

And because it's kid friendly, it's one of the best "go to" oils that you can have around.

## Blending with Bergamot

Clove
Geranium
Ginger
Frankincense
Sweet orange
Jasmine
Lavender
Lemon
Lime
Palmarosa
Peppermint
Rose
Rose geranium
Rosemary
Tea tree
Vetiver

# Cedarwood
## *Cedrus atlantica*

## Quick Start
Bass note
Family: Pinaceae
Extraction method: steam distilled
Country of origin: Morocco, Algeria
Price range: moderately priced
Safety notes:
Not for children, especially under age 5
Avoid use during pregnancy
Possible skin irritant- use diluted; do a patch test first.
Be sure to use cedarwood respectfully. Use cedarwood for a short time and then stop using it for a week or two before going back to using it again, if needed.

The cedarwood that's more commonly known as *Juniperus virginiana* is safe for children and child friendly.

## Practical Tips and uses for Cedarwood
One of the more interesting things about cedarwood is that it has the ability to thin mucus. I have an exciting little personal anecdote for you.
When I was formulating a sinus blend for myself, I tried many various oil combinations before I came up with a blend that worked for me consistently.
The winning blend included cedarwood. What this oil does is thin out the mucus in the nasal passages.

Practical application: a facial steam. During this procedure, basically everything just slides out of the nose and into the bowl of water. You would blow your nose and then continue with the steam. It's a little bit disgusting, but it works quite well. If you ever want to try it for that reason I think you'd be pleasantly surprised.

# Cedarwood
## *Cedrus atlantica*

Cedarwood is **antiseptic** and widely used in skin care, particularly for men.

Since cedarwood is a tree, men tend to find it much more pleasant to have on their skin rather than some floral oils. Cedarwood is very popular in men's **skin care** products for this reason.

It's also used in **hair growth formulas,** especially for men.

Cedarwood is an **insect repelling** oil, and is used often in insect repelling essential oil blends.

It is also **anti-fungal.** Cedarwood is used in preparations for skin conditions such as **eczema and psoriasis,** or **acne** and **blemishes.**

Cedarwood is very good for **stress, tension, anxiety** and **insomnia.** It's useful to have cedarwood in a massage oil blend for this purpose.

**Blending with Cedarwood**

Bergamot
Cypress
Frankincense
Geranium
Jasmine
Juniper berry
Lavender
Lemon
Patchouli
Pine
Rosemary
Rose
Spruce

# Chamomile, Roman
## *Anthemis nobilis L, Chamaemelum nobile*

## Quick Start
Middle note
Family: Compositae
Extraction method: steam distilled
Country of origin: United Kingdom
Price range: expensive
Safety notes:
Very suitable for children and babies
Pregnancy friendly after first trimester
Avoid using this oil if you have an allergy to ragweed

Roman chamomile used to be reasonably priced but it is not any more. Recently it has become very popular, and due to increased demand, chamomile has skyrocketed in price.
If you can afford to budget for this oil, however, I do recommend it, especially if you have small children.

## Practical Tips and uses for Roman Chamomile
Chamomile may have got it's claim to fame (or at least popularity) for it's value as a calming oil. It's very **calming** and **settling** to children, and helps them to sleep better.

Chamomile remains a parental favorite because you can use it to help tame the infamous toddler tantrum.
In fact, any **meltdowns and upsets** are lessened. This even applies to **nightmares** in children. Chamomile is one of the oils that I use when I make my Monster Spray because it's so helpful for calming down children who are upset.

Roman chamomile is good for **stress, anxiety** and **tension** as well. It is used for treating **headaches** and also **teething pain** (topically on the skin along the jawline).

# Chamomile, Roman
## *Anthemis nobilis L, Chamaemelum nobile*

Since chamomile is anti-inflammatory, it is useful to put in a blend for **sore muscles, aches** and **pains**. Chamomile is excellent to use in a first aid situation. Try it in a compress for aches and **sprains** and **strains**.

If you have small children who have an **upset tummy,** you can use chamomile in a massage oil blend for them. Chamomile is good for helping to relieve colic as well.

Chamomile isn't only for children. You can use it to ease **premenstrual symptoms,** too.

If you've got an **itchy, inflamed skin** condition like psoriasis and eczema, try chamomile.

**Did you know?**
There is more than one type of chamomile. There is also: German chamomile, Moroccan chamomile and cape chamomile. They are each a little different from one another, but for the purposes of this book, we will only be discussing Roman chamomile.

**Blending with Roman Chamomile**

Bergamot
Clary sage
Eucalyptus
German chamomile
Geranium
Moroccan chamomile
Lavender
Lemon
Mandarin
Myrrh
Orange, sweet
Patchouli
Rose
Vetiver
Ylang ylang

# Eucalyptus
## *Eucalyptus globulus*

## Quick Start
Top note
Family: Myrtaceae
Extraction method: steam distilled
Country of origin: Australia, China
Price range: inexpensive to reasonably priced
Safety notes:
Suitable for older children
Pregnancy friendly after first trimester
Never ingest this oil- it can be potentially fatal
Avoid if you have high blood pressure or have epilepsy
Dilute this oil before applying topically to your skin
Keep eucalyptus out of the reach of children!

## Practical Tips and uses for Eucalyptus
Eucalyptus is an energetic, sharp and lively oil, not to mention a very powerful one. There are many varieties of eucalyptus available, such as *eucalyptus radiata* as well as *eucalyptus smithii*. For the purposes of this book we will focus on *eucalyptus globulus*.

There are lots of reasons to get excited about using eucalyptus. It is full of personality, full of life, and a very hard worker. Eucalyptus is useful to have as part of a blend for **arthritic pain** or **muscle pain**.

Eucalyptus is also **antiseptic**, which makes it an excellent oil to have in your first aid kit. It's good for cleaning out wounds, and **disinfecting** them to make sure they do not become infected. Be sure to use a carrier oil when applying this oil topically.

# Eucalyptus
## *Eucalyptus globulus*

Eucalyptus is a favorite to have on hand during cold and flu time. It's highly **anti-viral** and you can use it in a blend to put in your diffuser, or make a spray so that you can disinfect hard surface areas such as countertops and doorknobs.

Eucalyptus is also a **decongestant** and an **expectorant**. Eucalyptus is excellent for diffuser use, but if you do not have a diffuser, you could place some in the shower for an aromatic steam treatment.

Eucalyptus can also can help with **headaches**, particularly if you blend it with peppermint and lavender.

Eucalyptus is also a main ingredient in **lice control** for the hair- it is often used with tea tree for this purpose.

Eucalyptus is **clearing and focusing,** helping you to complete your tasks.

**Blending with Eucalyptus**

Cedarwood
Geranium
Ginger
Juniper berry
Lavender
Lemon
Marjoram
Orange
Peppermint
Pine
Rosemary
Spearmint
Tea tree
Thyme

# Geranium
## *Pelargonium graveolens*

## Quick Start
Middle note
Family: Geraniaceae
Extraction method: steam distilled
Country of origin: China, Egypt, Morocco, South Africa
Price range: moderately priced
Safety notes:
Pregnancy friendly after first trimester
Dilute this oil before applying topically to your skin, especially if you have sensitive skin- a patch test is recommended.

Quick fact: geranium has its own botanical family!

## Practical Tips and uses for Geranium
Geranium is an interesting oil to me. It's one that I would select especially for women. Geranium, although it's so powerful, it has a soft edge, which makes it particularly suitable for women. Geranium has a soft, nurturing side. If I had to pick three oils for women it would be one of my top three. The other oils I would choose are rose and petitgrain.

One practical use for geranium is that it is **balancing** to the adrenals. When the body is under stress, the adrenals also experience stress, and can become fatigued, leading to other issues such as thyroid imbalance.

Geranium is **antidepressant** and **uplifting.** I often include it in blends for anxiety and stress.

It's **cleansing, anti-septic** and **toning,** making it an outstanding choice for skin care products. Geranium is suitable for all skin types, except very sensitive skin.

# Geranium
## *Pelargonium graveolens*

Geranium has anti candida properties, and is **anti-fungal**. You could also include tea tree in a blend for this purpose.

Since geranium is **hormone balancing**, it's very good for premenstrual (PMS) symptoms and menopausal symptoms, including those wretched mood swings.

Geranium is highly, highly aromatically potent. This is a kind way of saying that geranium can be a little on the stinky side. Ironically, this makes it really useful to use as an **insect repellent**. I like to blend it with patchouli for this purpose.

**Quick Tip:**
*Rose geranium* is an essential oil that is made by distilling rose petals along with geranium petals.
Rose geranium is a co-distilled oil.

Co-distilled oils are gaining popularity, as this method allows for more creative ideas.

**Blending with Geranium**

Bergamot
Black pepper
Other citrus
Clary sage
Clove bud
Jasmine
Lavender
Lemon
Neroli
Patchouli
Rose geranium
Vetiver

# Ginger Root
*Zingiber officinale*

## Quick Start
Top note- or bottom note, depending on who you ask
Family: Ziniberaceae
Extraction method: steam distilled, $CO_2$ extracted
Country of origin: China, Southern Asia
Price range: moderately priced
Safety notes:
Pregnancy friendly after first trimester- inhalation is fine when using for nausea
Not for use on children under age 5
Dilute this oil before applying topically to your skin, especially if you have sensitive skin- a patch test recommended
Ginger is slightly phototoxic- topical use for night time only.
Ginger is an anticoagulant, which means that it thins the blood. Stop using it two weeks before you have surgery of any kind plus two weeks after your surgery is over.

## Practical Tips and uses for Ginger Root
Ginger root is an essential oil that I really have come to depend upon. I don't leave home without it. Ginger is an oil that I would strongly urge you to have in your home basic care kit.

One of the most noted and useful things about ginger is its value for **pain management.** Try it for arthritic pain, muscle pain, muscle fatigue, cramping (including menstrual cramps).

Ginger root is known as a **circulatory aid**. It's a **warming** oil, so if you are cold, using ginger as part of your massage oil blend can help to warm your body.

Ginger root is also known as a good **digestive aid**.

# Ginger Root
## *Zingiber officinale*

To ease an upset tummy, dilute some ginger into a carrier oil of your choice, and apply topically.

Ginger is useful for cases of **nausea**. This could be pregnancy induced nausea, motion sickness, or even chemotherapy induced nausea. The best application in nausea cases is direct inhalation.

Ginger root is also an **antiseptic**. You could use it as part of your skincare routine, particularly if you have acne or blemishes. Ginger hydrosol would be my choice as a toner for night time use.

Ginger root is **anti-viral**. Adding ginger root to your blend of essential oils for cold and flu season can help banish those nasty germs.

Ginger also has a reputation as an **aphrodisiac**. Use it in a romantic massage oil blend with other oils such as neroli and cardamom. Ginger is emotionally grounding.

**Pro tip**: Try ginger and geranium in a facial steam for soothing a sore throat.

### Blending with Ginger Root

Bergamot
Cardamom
Cassummunar ginger
Cedarwood
Cinnamon
Galangal
Grains of paradise
Lavender
Lemon
Lime
Neroli
Orange
Patchouli
Petitgrain
Rosemary
Rosewood
Ylang ylang

# Lavender
*Lavandula angustifolia*

## Quick Start
Middle note
Family: Labiatae
Extraction method: steam distilled
Price range: moderately priced
Country of origin: France, South Africa, Bulgaria, Canada, USA
Safety notes:
Pregnancy friendly after first trimester
Child and baby friendly, suitable for the elderly and frail
Dilution of lavender is recommended in order to reduce the risk of sensitization
Generally a very safe and well tolerated oil

## Practical Tips and uses for lavender
Lavender is one of the best and well-loved essential oils in the world. It's extremely versatile, and it's a must have for your aromatherapy tool kit. There are hundreds of types of lavender, but to keep it simple, we will explore the widely available *Lavandula angustifolia*, and one that you are likely familiar with already.

Lavender is an extremely versatile oil. Lavender is an **analgesic.** It can be used to ease an **insect sting or bite.** It's **anti-fungal, antiseptic**, and is also calming and balancing.

Lavender has been widely used in **treating burns,** including radiation burns, sunburns and chemical burns. Mixing the lavender into an aloe gel is even more soothing and effective.

Lavender is widely used in **skincare** formulations as well. It is used for treating acne, as well as for treating scars.
Lavender is suitable for all skin types.

# Lavender
## *Lavandula angustifolia*

It may be used to help treat **eczema and psoriasis**.

Lavender is effective as an **insect repellent** as well, especially for use in insect repellent blend for children and babies.

Lavender is also a widely known **sleep aid**. In fact, studies have been done on the effectiveness of lavender as a sleep aid compared with prescribed medications. One thing I tell my clients when they are using lavender as a sleep aid, is that if you find it's working well for you, and then one day it stops working, just stop using it for a week or so and then try it again. This allows your body to reset and it should become effective again.

**Quick tip**: Put a couple drops on a tissue and place it under your pillow case. You can also make a room spray ahead of time and spray your pillow area just before bed.

Lavender promotes **emotional well-being** and **relaxation**. Lavender is an excellent oil to use during massage for this reason, as it helps to relax tense muscles.

## Blending with Lavender

Lavender blends with most other essential oils, but particularly:

Jasmine
Neroli
Rose
Oakmoss
Vetiver
Patchouli
Frankincense

**Quick Tip:**
Lavender is a good oil to put in your blend if you need to balance out or round off your blend aroma.

**Pro Tip:**
Use lavender in small amounts as a sleep aid. If you use too much lavender at one time, it can have the opposite effect and keep you awake.

# Marjoram, Sweet
*Marjorana hortensis, Origanum majorana*

## Quick Start
Middle note
Family: Labiatae
Extraction method: steam distilled
Country of origin: Egypt
Price range: moderately priced
Safety notes:
Avoid using during pregnancy
Avoid using marjoram if you suffer from depression, as this oil
is extremely sedative and may affect you adversely
Avoid using marjoram if you suffer from low blood pressure
If you have asthma, don't use it during an asthma attack


## Practical Tips and uses for sweet marjoram
Marjoram is a very useful essential oil to have as part of your
aromatherapy toolkit. Some practical uses for marjoram include
analgesic properties. It helps to deal with **muscle aches, muscle
pains** and **muscle cramps,** including menstrual cramps.

Marjoram is an antioxidant, a benefit if you want to use it in
your **skincare** preparations. It is also antiseptic, making it
handy for cleansing.

One of the things that I use marjoram for is as a **sleep aid.** It's a
sedative oil, and useful for insomnia. In fact, I recommend that
you don't attempt activities which require your complete
attention and focus while using it.

Marjoram is also helpful to have on hand to deal with
**headaches** and **migraines,** especially premenstrual tension
(PMT) headaches.

# Marjoram, Sweet
*Marjorana hortensis, Origanum majorana*

I include marjoram in blends that deal with **stress, anxiety** and **tension.** It is especially useful if you are holding a lot of tension and need to release it.
Try using sweet marjoram in a massage blend for that purpose.

People also use marjoram to help mellow **ADD** and **ADHD.**

It is also **blood pressure lowering (hypotensive).** If you already struggle with low pressure, avoid using sweet marjoram.

Alternatively, if you have high blood pressure, you could use sweet marjoram to help lower it.

Another thing I appreciate about marjoram is its **immune boosting** capabilities. It allows the body to sweat. When your body is sweating, it helps to unload all the toxins that are locked in and help move them out.

Marjoram also helps **respiratory** conditions, including colds and flu, asthma, and even bronchitis.

## Blending with Sweet Marjoram

Bergamot
Cedarwood
Chamomile
Clary sage
Cypress
Eucalyptus
Juniper berry
Lavender
Patchouli
Petitgrain
Vetiver
Rose
Rosemary
Tea tree
Thyme

# Orange, Sweet
## *Citrus sinensis*

## Quick Start
Top note- Middle note
Family: Rutaceae
Extraction method: cold pressed
Country of origin: Italy, USA, Israel, Brazil
Price range: inexpensive
Safety notes:
Pregnancy friendly and child friendly
Do a patch test on sensitive skin before topical application for the first time
Do not apply oxidized orange oil to the skin
Sweet orange is not phototoxic

## Practical Tips and uses for sweet orange
Sweet orange is one of my top picks for kids. I definitely recommend it as a must have for your aromatherapy toolkit.

Orange is a fun-loving oil. It's happy; it's uplifting and very cheerful. It is a lovely, giving oil. Some preschools use orange essential oil to make their own **sensory Play-Doh**. It helps the children to maintain a happy spirit while they are learning.

You could use orange as a **disinfectant** as part of your household cleaners. Blended with other citrus essential oils, you would have a refreshing aroma for the bathroom.

It's also a **decongestant,** often used for treating children with a cold or an illness during the winter months.

One of my favorite ways to use orange is as a **digestive aid**. One simple and effective thing that you can do if you have an

# Orange, Sweet
### *Citrus sinensis*

upset tummy is make a massage oil blend using orange and your choice of carrier oil. Simply rub it on your tummy until it is absorbed. You may be surprised at how quickly it calms an upset tummy, even for adults.

One thing that is not widely known about orange is that it is a **lymphatic stimulant**.
It encourages the removal of cellular debris and is a diuretic. Sweet orange becomes a very effective member of a blend for lymphatic massage, particularly if you combine it with grapefruit, which is also a lymphatic stimulant.

Orange goes beautifully in the diffuser, and you can use it in a room spray as well.

## Pro Tip:
One of my favorite combinations for orange is to mix it with frankincense and patchouli.

## Quick Tip:
Citrus oils in general are good digestion aids.

## Blending with Sweet Orange

When blending orange, you'll notice that it goes with all the **other citrus:**
Bergamot
Lime
Lemon

It also goes with these **spices:**
Cardamom
Cinnamon
Clove
Ginger

**as well as:**
Geranium
Lavender
Patchouli
Rosemary
Frankincense

# Peppermint
*Mentha piperita*

## Quick Start
Middle note
Family: Labiatae
Extraction method: steam distilled
Country of origin: India, USA, South Africa
Price range: moderately priced
Safety notes:
Not for use on small children under five years old
Avoid use during pregnancy and with nursing mothers
(it has been known to dry up the mother's milk supply)
Possible skin irritant, use diluted
Avoid if you have acid reflux
Store away from homeopathic remedies

## Practical Tips and uses for peppermint
Peppermint is a stimulating, fresh and lively essential oil. One of the most effective uses of peppermint is **pain management**. Many massage therapists use peppermint at the end of their treatment because it helps to deaden the pain that they've just put you through during your massage.

Another use for peppermint is as a **digestive aid.**
**Pro tip**: Smelling peppermint out of the bottle is actually more effective in easing a tummy upset than to drink peppermint tea, believe it or not. All you really have to do- is just smell it.

Peppermint is useful as an **antiviral** as well as an **expectorant**. During cold and flu season, add peppermint into into one of your blends to help fight off viruses that are coming your way. It also helps dislodge any mucus that is building up and move it out. Try a few drops in the shower for an invigorating aromatherapy treatment.

# Peppermint
### *Mentha piperita*

Peppermint is traditionally used for **headaches**. You may find recipes that suggest applying peppermint neat, but I recommend diluting it first, as I would do with any essential oil.

Peppermint has also been used to ease **itchy skin conditions**. If you have skin such as eczema or psoriasis it can be helpful to put it into one of your lotion bases or ointments.

Adding peppermint to a facial steam can help treat **acne**- and sinus and headache issues, too.

Rodents apparently do not like peppermint. All you have to do is put a few drops of peppermint onto several cotton balls and place them strategically around areas of your home to serve as a **pest deterrent**.

Since peppermint is **cooling** you can use it to reduce fever or hot flashes. The best way to use this is in a room or body spray application.

Many people find peppermint too **stimulating** to use at night- unless your goal is to stay awake.

Try it for jet lag.

## Blending with Peppermint

Bergamot
Cornmint
Cypress
Eucalyptus
Geranium
Lavender
Lemon
Lemongrass
Marjoram
Petitgrain
Pine
Spearmint
Rosemary
Tea tree

# Rosemary
*Rosmarinus officinalis*

## Quick Start
Middle note
Family: Labiatae
Extraction method: steam distilled
Country of origin: Spain
Price range: moderately priced
Safety notes:
Use with caution during pregnancy (reduced dilution rate)
Avoid use on children under age 5
Use with caution if you have high blood pressure
Avoid rosemary if you have epilepsy
Store away from homeopathic remedies
Possible skin irritant; use diluted

## Practical Tips and uses for rosemary
Rosemary is one of my favorite essential oils because it is so versatile. It's very accessible and it's a wonderful oil, one that I recommend for your toolkit at home.

Some of the special talents of rosemary include it's **toning** abilities. For this reason, rosemary is widely used in skin care preparations, particularly for mature skin. It helps to regenerate skin tissue and it also helps to tighten slack skin. It's also **cleansing**.
Rosemary is often used to treat acne and blemishes.

Rosemary is **antibacterial**. Many blends make use rosemary, especially ones that are for use during cold or flu season. Using rosemary in the hospitals reduced instances of infection. It is a powerful **disinfectant**.

Rosemary is a **decongestant**. You can use it in diffuser to help clear anything respiratory, including sinus or cold issues.

# Rosemary
## *Rosmarinus officinalis*

Rosemary is a very **stimulating** oil, so my advice is to not use it at nighttime, unless you want to stay awake. However, rosemary is a perfect choice for use in the morning to get started.

Rosemary is known to **promote hair growth**, and it's often used in hair growth formulas for men and women alike. You can add some rosemary into your shampoo, or perhaps in a hair oil treatment. Rosemary promotes hair growth by stimulating the hair follicles and increasing circulation to the area.

Rosemary has a **warming action** on the body and on the muscles, and stimulates local **circulation**. Try it for sore muscles or cramps.

One thing I find interesting about rosemary is that it helps the body unload waste by **stimulating the lymphatic system**, a body system often under-appreciated.

One of the most well known applications of rosemary is for **memory recall**. You've heard the saying "Rosemary for remembrance". There's a reason for this. Seniors and students alike use rosemary.

## Blending with Rosemary

Bergamot
Cedarwood
Lemon
Lavender
Lemongrass
Peppermint, mints
Sweet orange

### Quick Start:
There are different rosemary chemotypes. I think of them as having their own individual personalities. When you are making your selection for purchase, the label may have the letters **CT.** This stands for chemotype, and it will indicate that specific chemotype for that rosemary:

CT 1,8-cineole
CT borneol
CT camphor
CT limonene

# Tea Tree
*Melaleuca alternifolia*

## Quick Start
Top note
Family: Myrtaceae
Extraction method: steam distilled
Country of origin: Australia, China
Price range: reasonably priced
Safety notes:
Tea tree is generally quite a safe essential oil
Child friendly and pregnancy friendly after the first trimester
Tea tree is one of the few oils that you can use neat, however, I recommend diluting it for topical use in most cases
Possible skin irritant to sensitive skin (especially applied neat)

## Practical Tips and uses for tea tree
Tea tree is a versatile powerhouse. Claims to fame include having **anti-fungal, anti-septic, antiviral, and anti-bacterial** properties. There are many opportunities for using tea tree in a first aid situation or for medicinal purposes.

Tea tree is an **immune stimulant, expectorant and decongestant,** making it an excellent oil to have during cold and flu season. Try it as part of your diffuser blend, or in a massage oil blend.

Tea tree is also **anti-inflammatory,** making it a good choice for a body massage oil for pain and inflammation.

Since tea tree is anti-bacterial, it is widely used for treating **acne** and **blemishes.** Try it on a q-tip mixed with some jojoba or grapeseed oil and apply directly to the pimple. You could also make your blend and put it into a rollerball for easy application. Adding lavender or sandalwood is nice, too.

# Tea Tree
## *Melaleuca alternifolia*

Tea tree **eases burns** (including sunburn), and is especially effective when blended with lavender. Combine with a water based cream or lotion containing aloe vera for added benefit.

Tea tree may be used in ointments and creams for treating **cradle cap** and **diaper rash**. Try blending with lavender or chamomile.

## Quick Tip:

One thing that you should know about tea tree is that it has a slightly shorter shelf life than some of the other essential oils.
I recommend purchasing it in smaller quantities so that you can have a chance to use it up before it goes off. If it does go off, don't try to use it on your skin, but you can use it in a room spray, or cleaning solution of your choice.

## Pro Tip:

One of my favorite blends for tea tree includes sandalwood and lavender. I blend these into a quality unscented cream base to make a quick hand cream.

## Blending with Tea Tree

Chamomiles
Clove
Eucalyptus
Geranium
Juniper berry
Lavender
Lemon
Marjoram
Myrrh
Oregano
Peppermint
Pine
Rosemary
Sandalwood
Ylang ylang

# Carrier Oils

# Carrier Oils

Carrier oils are an interesting study apart from essential oils. Since you should be purchasing at least one or two for your aromatherapy toolkit, here is a listing of some of the most versatile and accessible carrier oils at different price points. Try to purchase organic oils wherever possible.
And- Never put carrier oils into your diffuser!

## Basic: use at 100%
These may be used alone as a base oil, or blended, if desired.

**Sunflower Oil** (*Helianthus annuus*)
- suitable for all skin types
- excellent for massage
- helps heal blemishes and scar tissue

**Grapeseed** (*Vitis vinifera*)
- suitable for all skin types, especially oily and combination skin (slightly astringent)
- good as a massage oil

**Rice Bran** (*Oryza sativa*)
- suitable for all skin types, even sensitive skin
- suitable for babies and children
- has a quick absorption rate, making it a good choice for face oils

**Sweet Almond Oil** (*Prunus dulcis*)
- excellent for dry and mature skin (emollient)
- do not use this oil if you have a nut allergy
- excellent for massage
- has anti-inflammatory properties
- has anti-fungal properties

# Carrier Oils

## Nice to have: use at 30-70%
These carrier oils may be a little expensive to use alone, but are worth having, especially as an additive to your massage oil blend.

**Jojoba** (*Simmondsia chinensis*)
- suitable for all skin types
- jojoba is technically not an oil, but a liquid wax
- jojoba molecular structure closely resembles that of human skin

**Apricot Kernel** (*Prunus armeniaca*)
- suitable for all skin types, especially mature skin
- apricot kernel has re-hydrating qualities
- add this oil into a salve for mild eczema

**Avocado** (*Persea gratissima*)
- this is a little heavier oil; best mixed with a lighter oil such as any of the basic oils
- nourishing to dry skin (excellent emollient), penetrates skin layers more deeply
- helps to repair damaged skin

**Sesame** (*Sesamum indicum*)
- do not purchase sesame oil from the grocery store or you will smell like takeout food-purchase from your essential oil supplier instead
- sesame oil has a natural SPF of about 4
- widely used in natural health and beauty applications

**Safflower** (*Carthamus tinctorius*)
- used as a hair growth treatment
- used in skin care for acne, and also mature skin

# Carrier Oils

**Specialty: use at 3-10%**
These carrier oils are generally more expensive and may be used in a lower dilution compared with the rest of the oils in your base oil blend.

**Argan** (*Argania Spinosa*)
- used globally for hair, body and skin care products
- has extensive nourishing properties
- supply and demand has driven the price of this oil up

**Evening Primrose** (*Oenothera biennis*)
- use as an additive to your base oil
- avoid use during pregnancy
- excellent benefits for mature skin

**Hemp Seed** (*Cannabis sativa*)
*does not contain the substances that will make one "high"
- very nourishing to dry skin
- may be added to your massage oil base for pain
- good for skin conditions such as eczema and psoriasis

**Raspberry Seed** (*Rubus idaeus*)
- has a natural SPF of 30 and high levels of vitamin C
- this is a very expensive oil

**Rosehip Seed** (*Rosa Canina, Rosa Rubiginosa*)
- excellent for mature skin
- known as a skin regenerating oil

**Sea Buckthorn** (*Hippophae rhamnoides*)
- known for treating skin conditions, injuries and ailments

# Carrier Oils

## Herbal Infused Oils (macerated)

Infused oils are a valuable asset to your carrier oil stash. Many of them are accessible from reputable suppliers, with the following list being the most common ones. If you are so inclined, you can also make your own herbal oils. Olive, almond and sunflower oils are often used because they remain stable during the infusion process.

**Arnica** (*Arnica montana*)
- traditionally used for pain
- increases circulation to local area
- do not apply this oil to open wounds

**Calendula** (*Calendula officinalis*)
- a natural choice for healing old wounds, scars, etc.
- use it on damaged or burned skin
- excellent additive to ointments

**Carrot Seed** (*Beta carotene*)
- deeply nourishing to skin, free radical scavenger
- may help to reduce scars
- add this to your blend at 10%

**St. John's Wort** (*Hypericum perforatum*)
- used on areas of nerve damage
- add at 25% to your massage oil blend for stress
- used to heal skin from burns and sun damage

## For instructions on how to make infused herbal oils:

https://naturenote.ca/2017/03/13/how-to-make-infused-herbal-oil/

# Recipes

# Recipes for children

## Quick Start
*Please note: the following recipes may need to be adjusted for use on children (if applicable), pregnant and/or nursing mothers, and the elderly or frail.

Also be sure to take into consideration any oils which are contra-indicated for you, or not suitable for your use.

## Quick Tip:
Be sure to take into consideration the best method for use:

• diffuser or nebulizer
• massage blend
• bath oil
• room spray
• perfume
• facial steam
• etc.

## Monster Spray
4oz or 120ml distilled water
16 drops lavender
16 drops mandarin
8 drops sweet marjoram
8 drops Roman chamomile

Add the drops together into a suitable container with a spray mist top. Add the water and allow to mix for 24 hours. Shake gently before each use.

## Make Me Happy Massage Oil
3oz or 90ml grapeseed oil
1oz or 30ml apricot kernel oil
2 capsules 400 UI vitamin e
32 drops sweet orange
16 drops petitgrain

Add the carrier oils together. Add the essential oils into the carrier oils, one drop at a time. Pierce the vitamin e capsules with a sterilized pin and add to the mix.
Using a clean chopstick, stir to blend. Transfer to a 4oz or 120ml bottle with a suitable cap.
This is lovely for after bath and before bed time as a massage oil. It can be applied to an upset tummy as well.

# Blends for children

## Snuffle Buster EO Blend
3 drops tea tree
3 drops eucalyptus
3 drops lavender

## Sunshine EO Blend
2 drops lavender
3 drops lemon
3 drops grapefruit

## Feel Better Soon EO Blend
2 drops lemon
1 drop ginger root
2 drops sweet orange

## Citrus EO Blend
5 drops bergamot
5 drops sweet orange
5 drops lemon
5 drops grapefruit

## Sleepy Time EO Blend
2 drops myrtle
2 drops lavender
2 drops mandarin

## Study Time EO Blend
2 drops frankincense
2 drops sweet orange
2 drops rosemary

## Other nice combinations:
lavender + tea tree

eucalyptus + tea tree

dill + fennel + sweet orange

frankincense + sweet orange

chamomile + lavender

## Quick Start
Did you know that you can add hydrosols to your diffuser?
This is an excellent alternative if your child has aroma sensitivities, but you still want to have a subtle aromatic treatment.
Be sure to use pure hydrosols without any added chemicals.

Hydrosols to try:
• Cornflower
• Lavender
• Lemon balm
• Neroli
• Rose

# Kid's Corner

## Suggested essential oils for children

Always do a skin patch test before using your blend over the child's whole body.
Do not let your child ingest any oils.

## Dilution rates:

### Babies 2-6 months
use: 0.5%
dilution rate
1-2 drops in 30ml/1oz

### Babies 6-12 months
use: 0.5%
dilution rate
1-4 drops in 30ml/1oz

### Children ages 1-5
years use: 0.5% to 1.0%
dilution rate
5-8 drops in 30ml/1oz

### Children ages 6-14
years use: 1 to 1.5%
dilution rate
5-12 drops in 30ml/1oz

## Oils for babies from 2-6 months
Roman, German chamomiles
Yarrow
Dill
Lavender
Neroli
Mandarin
Rose

## Oils for babies 6-12 months
The oils listed above, plus:
Palmarosa
Tea tree
Coriander
Grapefruit

## Oils for children aged 1-5 years
The oils listed above, plus:
1/3 dose Ginger root
Myrtle

## Oils for children aged 6-14 years
(After age 12, these oils may be used at full dosage.)
The oils listed above, plus:
Frankincense
Cajeput
Cypress
Spearmint
Marjoram
Eucalyptus

# Kid's Corner

Although especially suitable for children, these essential oils are helpful for big kids too. Keep in mind the correct dilution rate for the age of your child, and which are suitable for your child's age range. Choose a single oil for young children, or create a blend using 2-3 oils for older children.

**Anger**
Lavender
Bergamot
Roman chamomile

**Fear**
Roman chamomile
Frankincense

**Anxiety**
Lavender
Mandarin
Geranium
Marjoram

**Hyperactive**
Mandarin

**Tantrums**
Roman chamomile

**Self esteem**
Grapefruit
Bergamot

**Sleep**
Lavender
Marjoram

**Comforting**
Sweet orange
Bergamot

**Concentration**
Peppermint
Rosemary
Frankincense
Geranium

**Oils for children aged 6-14 years cont'd.**
The following essential oils may be used, but at 1/3 the dose.

| | | |
|---|---|---|
| peppermint | rosemary | clary sage |
| benzoin | thyme (linalool) | geranium |

**What do I mean by 1/3 dose?**
These oils should not exceed more than one third of your total blend of essential oils.

# Massage Oil Blends

## Woodland massage oil
3 drops cedarwood
3 drops eucalyptus
3 drops sweet orange
1 drop fir balsam
Add to:
4 tsp or 20ml base oil blend

This recipe should make 1-2 applications.
This blend is uplifting, restorative and refreshing.
Avoid during pregnancy.

## Relaxing massage oil
3 drops thyme (linalool)
3 drops lavender
3 drops lime
1 drop patchouli
Add to:
4 tsp or 20ml base oil blend
This recipe should make 1-2 applications.
This blend is deeply relaxing and grounding.
Avoid during pregnancy.
Avoid exposure to sun for 12 hours (or use steam distilled lime instead of cold pressed).

## Base oil blend for massages
Mix up the following to have on hand for when you want to make a massage oil.

Makes 250 ml or just over 8.45 oz

200ml or 6.7 oz sunflower oil
40ml or 1.35 oz apricot kernel oil
10ml or 0.33 oz jojoba
4 capsules vitamin e 400 UI

Keep a note of the expiry dates on your carrier oils. Your mix should be stable at least as far as the most recent expiry date.

## Using infused herbal oils
If you have access to herbal oils such as calendula, arnica, carrot tissue, comfrey or St. John's wort, you can add them into your base oil blend as a replacement for the apricot kernel oil.

For step by step instructions on how to make your own herbal infused oils, check out this link:

https://naturenote.ca/2017/03/13/how-to-make-infused-herbal-oil/

# Massage Oil Blends

## Muscle rehab massage oil
4 drops rosemary
4 drops eucalyptus
2 drops peppermint
2 drops juniper berry
Add to:
4 tsp or 20ml base oil blend

This recipe should make 1-2 applications.
This blend helps to promote circulation, and reduce inflammation and promote recovery from physical workouts.
Avoid during pregnancy.

## Citrus dream massage oil
2 drops lime
6 drops tangerine
2 drops cardamom
6 drops sweet orange
6 drops bergamot
6 drops petitgrain
8 drops rosewood
Add to:
2oz or 60ml base oil blend

This recipe should make many applications.
This blend promotes feelings of wellbeing and relaxation.
Avoid exposure to sun for 12 hours.

## Baby massage oil
2 drops lavender
1 drop Roman chamomile
Add to:
30ml or 1 oz rice bran oil
1 capsule vitamin e
Bottle with cap, suitable size- 30ml/1oz

This recipe should make several applications.
Try this blend after bath time and before bed. If the baby is fussing too much for a massage to be practical, try adding a small amount into the bath water instead.

# Room Spray Blends

## Focus
10 drops frankincense
5 drops vetiver
20 drops sweet orange
10 drops cedarwood
5 drops ylang ylang
120ml/4oz spray bottle
120ml/4oz distilled water

Mix the essential oils together, drop by drop into a suitable spray bottle with a mister cap. Add the distilled water, or a hydrosol if you choose.

This recipe may be adapted for use in a roller bottle. Switch out the water for 8ml of carrier oil of your choice. I usually use sunflower oil, or jojoba. Add in 1 capsule of vitamin e 400 UI.

This blend may also be adapted for use as a diffuser blend- use the essential oils only. Double the number of drops for each oil and store in a 5ml bottle.

## Good Cheer
20 drops bergamot
2 drops lemongrass
12 drops sweet orange
2 drops cinnamon
5 drops clove
2 drops coriander
3 whole cloves
120ml/4oz spray bottle
120ml/4oz distilled water

Mix the essential oils together, drop by drop into a suitable spray bottle with a mister cap. Add the distilled water, or a hydrosol if you choose.

This is a lovely room spray to have for festive occasions.

This blend may also be adapted for use as a diffuser blend- use the essential oils only. Double the number of drops for each oil and store in a 5ml bottle.

# Room Spray Blends

## Forest Breeze
8 drops juniper berry
8 drops bergamot
10 drops lemongrass
10 drops cedarwood
4 drops fir balsam
120ml/4oz spray bottle
120ml/4oz distilled water

Mix the essential oils together, drop by drop into a suitable spray bottle with a mister cap.
Add the distilled water, or a hydrosol if you choose.

Practical spaces for this blend would include the bathroom, kitchen, or any room that needs refreshing.

This blend may also be adapted for use as a diffuser blend- use the essential oils only.
Double the number of drops for each oil and store in a 5ml bottle.

## Mellow Out
10 drops lavender
10 drops bergamot
10 drops sw. marjoram
5 drops ylang ylang
2 drops Roman cham.
2 drops cardamom
120ml/4oz spray bottle
120ml/4oz distilled water

Mix the essential oils together, drop by drop into a suitable spray bottle with a mister cap.
Add the distilled water.

This blend may also be adapted for use as a massage oil blend. Be sure to consult the dilution calculation chart for your individual situation.

# Ointments & Balms

**Chamomile Herbal Salve**
4 oz extra virgin olive oil
2.5 oz sweet almond oil
0.5 oz infused calendula herbal oil
40g beeswax
10 drops lavender
5 drops Roman chamomile
2 drops neroli
3 capsules vitamin e

**Note**: You will need use the water bath method to make this recipe.

Weigh out the beeswax and place inside the water bath.

Measure out the olive, almond and calendula oils and add to the melting beeswax.

Continue to gently heat over low heat, stirring occasionally with a wooden implement.

When it is all in liquid form, remove from heat and set aside. Wait for about a minute, then add in the drops of essential oils. Pierce the vitamin e capsules and squeeze into the mixture.

Stir again until combined.

Pour immediately into waiting containers.

Makes about 7 ounces.

This herbal salve is suitable for babies. It may be used for cradle cap, upset tummy, and diaper rash. The beeswax provides a nice barrier, providing comfort and healing during diaper rash episodes.

This salve is also suitable for the elderly and frail.

**Quick Tip:**
You can adapt this recipe to formulate other ointments. Keep the total amount of oil the same, and the total amount of essential oil the same. You can also use your dilution chart to calculate a therapeutic (4-10%) dose for localized, targeted areas.

# Ointments & Balms

## Basic Lip Balm

31g shea butter
1 oz infused calendula oil
1 oz jojoba
1 capsule vitamin e

**Note:** You will need use the water bath method to make this recipe.

Weigh out the shea butter and place inside the water bath using an appropriately sized glass vessel.

Measure out the calendula oil and jojoba and add to the shea butter.

Continue to heat everything gently over low heat, stirring occasionally with a wooden implement.

When it is all in liquid form, remove from heat and set aside.

Wait for about a minute, then add in the vitamin e capsule by piercing it and squeezing it into the mixture.

Pour into suitable clean and dry containers.

This consistency of this lip balm can be adjusted by changing the amount of shea butter to make it more or less soft.

## Quick Start:

What is a water bath?

A water bath is a larger sized pot filled about halfway with water on the stove.
Another glass (and heat proof–such as Pyrex) measuring device with a pouring spout is placed into the water.
The ingredients are heated and melted together over medium low heat inside the glass vessel without ever touching the water. Usually, the mixture is transferred to ready (clean and dry) jars or containers.

# Lists of Top 10 essential oils

## Women

Lavender
Geranium
Rose
Jasmine
Clary sage
Neroli
Patchouli
Bergamot
Grapefruit
Tea tree

The oils in this list were chosen to provide the maximum care when dealing with issues that are common to women. This includes:
• stress
• anxiety
• hormonal issues
• muscle tension
• depression

## Men

Cedarwood
Pine
Patchouli
Bergamot
Cypress
Tea tree
Vetiver
Fir
Spruce
Eucalyptus

The oils in this list were chosen to provide the maximum care when dealing with issues that are common to men. This includes:
• stress
• anxiety
• muscle tension
• fatigue
• insomnia

A few years ago I conducted a clinical study on a small group of menopausal women aged 40-56 over 4 weeks. A blend of lavender, geranium and peppermint was given to each participant, as well as a spray bottle and massage oil base (with mixing instructions) so they could use the blend in whatever application suited their needs. Top results: reduction in headaches, insomnia, night sweats and constipation.

# Lists of Top 10 essential oils

## Children
Dill
Eucalyptus
Grapefruit
Roman chamomile
Lavender
Mandarin
Myrtle
Palmarosa
Ravensara
Tangerine

The list for children includes versatile oils that help deal with:
• upset tummy
• fear
• meltdowns
• illness

## Travel
Chamomile
Citronella
Clove
Ginger root
Lavender
Lemongrass
Peppermint
Sweet orange
Tea tree
Thyme (linalool type)

When traveling, in addition to your essential oils, it's also nice to have:
• carrier oil
• empty bottle or container to mix up what you need
• aloe vera gel
• witch hazel

## Startup Collection
Bergamot
Chamomile
Eucalyptus
Frankincense
Lemon
Lavender
Peppermint
Rosemary
Sweet marjoram
Tea tree

## Nice Extras
Cardamom
Carrot seed
Helichrysum
Jasmine
Melissa
Neroli
Rose
Rosalina
Sandalwood
Vetiver

# Equipment Lists

## Essential oil blending

• glass dark colored bottles in different sizes (5, 10 or 15ml sizes)

• measuring device: graduated glass cylinder (I have three of these- one is 25ml, and the other 2 are both 10ml)

• bottle brushes for cleaning the above

• different bottle closure types such as:
  • drip cap
  • dropper cap

• larger size dark glass bottles to hold a larger batch of a blend (30-50 ml sizes is good)

• pipettes

• pieces of card stock for blending perfumes

• labels for your blends

## Massage oil blending

• selected variety of suitable carrier oils, including a couple from the nice to have list (p. 87)

• glass measuring devices such as beakers or measuring cups with different markings:
  • teaspoons
  • tablespoons
  • mils
  • ounces
  • grams

• wooden stirring implement (I use a clean chopstick)

• small mixing dish large enough for a single application- preferably ceramic or glass

• vitamin E capsules to add to your massage oils to help extend the shelf life of the carrier oils

• selected variety of pure essential oils to add into your massage oil

• suitable bottle and closure for storage of your blend

• labels for your blends

# Equipment Lists

## Getting Organized: Practical tips

• have a binder or log book to keep charts for yourself and family members for whom you make blends

• keep a place for all your recipes and formulations in your binder or journal, including those "fails"

• keep a master list of all the oils you have, including the botanical name and estimated shelf life

• keep a master list of your favorite suppliers for:
  • essential oils
  • carrier oils
  • butters and waxes
  • hydrosols
  • containers and packaging
  • information and education

• arrange suitable and practical storage for your oils and hydrosols

• keep a shelf- or perhaps an entire bookcase- for your "aromatherapy library" books

## Other

• an accurate scale with a tare feature is always nice to have

• spray bottles with a mist cap come in handy for making room and body sprays

• roller bottles are a nice addition to your supply list, especially if you make perfumes

• ointment and lip balm tins in 2 oz sizes (60ml, 57g)

# Resources & Suppliers

**Australia**
International Aromatherapy and Aromatic Medicine (IAAMA)
http://www.iaama.org.au/

Stone Rise Farm
http://www.stonerisefarm.com/srffaq.html

New Directions Aromatics (Australia)
https://shop.newdirections.com.au/epages/newdirections.sf

**Canada**
Canadian Federation of Aromatherapists (CFA)
https://www.cfacanada.com/

British Columbia Alliance of Aromatherapy (BCAOA)
http://www.bcaoa.org/

Natural Oils Research Association (NORA)
http://www.cwhn.ca/en/node/15296

Rae Dunphy Aromatics Ltd.
http://www.raedunphy.ca/

Nature Notes Aromatherapy
https://naturenotes.ca/

**India**
Essential oil association of India (EOAI)
http://www.eoai.co.in/index.html

Kush Aroma Exports
https://www.kusharomaexports.com/

# Resources & Suppliers

**Thailand**
Herb Basics
http://www.herbbasicschiangmai.com/

**United Kingdom**
International Federation of Aromatherapists (IFA)
http://www.ifaroma.org/us/home/

Materia Aromatica
https://materiaaromatica.com/

Naissence Natural Healthy Living
https://www.enaissance.co.uk/essential-oils

**United States**
Alliance of International Aromatherapists (AIA)
https://www.alliance-aromatherapists.org/

National Association for Holistic Aromatherapy (NAHA)
https://naha.org/

Mountain Rose Herbs
https://www.mountainroseherbs.com/

Stillpoint Aromatics
https://stillpointaromatics.com/

# Glossary of Terms

**Analgesic-**soothes pain

**Anticoagulant-**thins the blood (prevents formation of clots)

**Antidepressant-**helps alleviate (minor) depression

**Antispasmodic-**eases spasms and cramps

**Antiphlogistic-**counteracts inflammation

**Antimicrobial-**resists or inhibits growth of pathogenic micro-organisms

**Anti-rheumatic-**helps ease rheumatism

**Antiseptic-**destroys and prevents microbial growth

**Antioxidant-**provides delay to cellular damage reducing aging of tissues

**Aromatherapy-** therapeutic use of essential oils (and hydrosols)

**Carminative-**relieves intestinal gas, bloating and flatulence

**Cautery-**promotes healing

**Chemotype-**the same botanical species occurring in other forms due to different growing conditions such as altitude, soil conditions, climate, etc.

**Cytophylactic-**promotes cell regeneration

**Decongestant-**reduces production and secretion of mucus

# Glossary of Terms

from the nasal passage

**Deodorant-**reduces odor

**Depurative-** helps to cleanse, purify and detoxify the blood and organs

**Diuretic-**helps to promote urine flow and output

**Emenagogue-**helps to induce or regulate menstruation

**Galactagogue-**increases milk secretion in nursing mothers

**Hepatic-** relates to the liver

**Hypotensive-**lowers blood pressure

**Hypertensive-**raises blood pressure

**Nervine-**has a balancing effect on the nervous system

**Rebefacient-**causes reddening of the skin due to localized circulation

**Sedative-**soothing, calming, causing reduction in activity

**Soporific-** induces sleep

**Sudorific-**promotes sweating

**Tonic-**strengthening and revitalizes the whole body, or may refer to a specific part of the body: ie. liver tonic

# Bibliography

Robert Tisserand & Rodney Young, Essential Oil Safety, (second edition) Churchill Livingstone, 2014

Jane Buckle, Clinical Aromatherapy 2nd Edition, Churchill Livingstone, 2003

Julia Lawless, The Encyclopedia of Essential Oils, Conari Press, 2013

Valerie Worwood, The Complete Book of Essential Oils & Aromatherapy, New World Library, 1991

Jennie Harding, The Essential Oils Handbook, Duncan Baid Publishers, 2008

Jean Valnet (Edited by Robert Tisserand), The Practice of Aromatherapy, C.W. Daniel Company, 1991

Gill Farrer-Halls, The Aromatherapy Bible, Sterling Publishing, 2005

Kurt Schnaubelt, The Healing Intelligence of Essential Oils, Healing Arts Press, 2011

Kathi Keville & Mindy Green, Aromatherapy- A Complete Guide to the Healing Art, Crossing Press, 2009

Maggie Tisserand, Aromatherapy for Women, Healing Arts Press, 1996

Denise Whichello Brown, Aromatherapy, Bookpoint Ltd., 2003

Beverly Hawkins, Aromatherapy 201, 2009

Peter & Kate Damian, Aromatherapy Scent & Psyche, Healing Arts Press, 1995

# Bibliography

Shirley Whitton, Essential Oils & Essences, New Burlington Books, Quintet Publishing Ltd., 1995

Nerys Purchon & Lora Cantele, The Complete Aromatherapy & Essential Oils handbook for everyday wellness, Robert Rose Inc., 2014

Dr. Scott A. Johnson, Evidence-Based Essential Oil Therapy: The ultimate guide to the therapeutic and clinical application of essential oils, Scott A. Johnson Professional Writing Services, LLC, 2015

Anna Huete, Aromatherapy: The healing power of plants and flowers, Konecky & Konecky, Old Saybrook, CT, 2007

Dr. Mariza Snyder, Smart mom's guide to essential oils, Ulysses Press, 2017

"What is aromatherapy?" Aromatherapy.com. Accessed 2018.http://www.aromatherapy.com/

Valerie Gennari Cooksley, Aromatherapy: Soothing Remedies to Restore, Rejuvenate and Heal, Prentice Hall Press, 2002

Jeane Rose, The aromatherapy book, Herbal studies course/Jeane Rose, San Fransisco, CA and Northern Atlantic books, Berkley CA, 1992

Len Price with Shirley Price, Carrier Oils for Aromatherapy and Massage, Riverhead Publishing, Stratford-upon-Avon, Warwickshire, England, 2008

Althea Press. Essential oils Natural Remedies: The Complete A-Z Reference of Essential Oils for Health and Healing. Berkeley, CA: Althea Press, 2015

# Index

Absolute, definition, 11,
  shelf life, 17
Almond oil, 86
Anger, oils for, 95
Anxiety, oils for, 95
Apricot kernel oil, 87
Aromatherapy, definition, 2,
  routes of application, 14, 15
Argan oil, 88
Arnica infused oil, 89
Avocado oil, 87
Base blend, 96
Bass notes, 56
Bergamot, 27, 33, 46, 48, **60-61**
Blending, wheel, 52
  tips, 53-57
Blood pressure, high, 34,
  low, 34
Botanical families, 48-49
Calendula infused oil, 89
Cancer care, 28-33
Carrier oils, definition, 5,
  examples, **85-89**, 93
Carrot infused oil, 89
Cedarwood, 27, 33, 44, 49, **62-63**
Chamomile, Roman, 32, 33, 46,
49, **64-65**
Chamomile herbal salve, 100
Choosing oils, 12
Citrus oils, 46
  shelf life, 16
Citrus EO blend, 93
Clinical aromatherapy,
  definition, 3

Co2, extraction, 11
  shelf life, 17
Cold pressed oils, 10
Comforting oils, 95
Concentration, oils for, 95
Contraindication chart, 38-40
Cost factors of oils, 8
Classification, 44-47
Diffuser, choosing, 14
Dilution rates, 40-41
Enfleurage, 11
Epilepsy, seizures, 34
Equipment lists, 104
Essential oils, definition, 4
Eucalyptus, 35, 44, 49, **66-67**
Extraction methods, 10-11
Extracts, 17
Evening primrose oil, 88
Feel better EO blend, 93
Focus spray, 98
Floral oils, 46
Geranium, 25, 33, 46, **68-69**
Ginger root, 27, 44, 48, **70-71**
Glaucoma, 34
Glossary of terms, 108-109
Grapeseed oil, 86
Gums and resins, 47
Hemp oil, 88
Make me happy massage oil, 92
High blood pressure, 34
Homeopathic remedies, 35
Hydrosols, definition, 10
Hyperactivity, oils for, 89
Ingestion of oils, 15,

# Index

CPSIA information can be obtained
at www.ICGtesting.com
Printed in the USA
LVHW03s1230260818
588080LV00008B/125/P